PONIES

by
Dorian Williams

DEAR JOHNNY
from
His very own
NANA
who
Loves Him
Always
x

Hamlyn
London·NewYork·Sydney·Toronto

x
EASTER 1972

CONTENTS

ACKNOWLEDGEMENTS

The publishers wish to thank the following for permission to reproduce the photographs used on the Cover, Roger Perry; Frontispiece, Camera Press; Front Endpaper, Thomas A. Wilkie; Back Endpaper, Tom Parker.

Other Acknowledgements, page 61

First Published 1971
Second Impression 1971

Published by The Hamlyn Publishing Group Limited
LONDON · NEW YORK · SYDNEY · TORONTO
Hamlyn House, Feltham, Middlesex, England
© Copyright The Hamlyn Publishing Group Limited, 1971
ISBN 0 600 34812 1
Printed by Litografia A. Romero, S. A.
Santa Cruz de Tenerife, Canary Islands

INTRODUCTION

You all know that there are many different breeds of horse. They are different sizes, colours, shapes, have different temperaments, and because of these differences, we use them for different purposes. In this book, we are going to show you pictures of some of the smaller breeds of horse, which are commonly known as ponies.

Ponies have a history of working alongside man. They have worked in coal mines and been part of circus menageries. Tinkers and gipsies have for generations relied on them to pull their carts and caravans.

For most people nowadays they mean sport and companionship. Thousands of children join Pony Clubs and many lucky children own ponies of their own and ride them at gymkhanas. Pony trekking is popular in places as far apart as Arizona and Argyll, or Australia and the moors of Yorkshire.

They are fascinating and lovable creatures. Although they have been domesticated, horses are by nature herd animals. There are still herds of wild ponies. In Great Britain they live in the New Forest and on Exmoor and Dartmoor.

Remember that horses and ponies have had to learn to trust man. They let man control them, think for them, tell them what to do and how to do it. Their trust must never be abused.

Away from his natural herd, a pony is nervous. So man must be gentle with him. He must never be hurried. People about him must be quiet, he will only bite or kick when he is frightened.

Horses have figured in myth and legend, and have been the subject of hundreds of poems and stories. We picture wild rides through the night to save a city, or a highwayman astride a pony on some lonely heath.

But for most of us a pony means a companion, a splendid mixture of muscle and bone, whether he is jumping at a gymkhana or standing alone in his paddock or running as a foal with his mother, when he has yet to feel the bit and the rein.

From the moment he is born a foal is ready to be friendly. Unlike a baby he can get up as soon as he is born. He looks around, finds out first where he can get his breakfast. Then he sees you. 'Hullo! What's this?' Tiny as he is, perhaps only an hour or two old, he is inquisitive – and cheeky! 'Let's see!' he says, and wobbling on unsteady legs he lurches towards you: sways a little and considers you. Not for one moment does he suspect that you might be a danger. Why should he? He has never met anything that might frighten him. And so he trusts everything – including you. If he is frightened, then it is your fault.

It is up to you to get his confidence, so that he will trust you, want to be friendly with you, even play with you. To be sure you get this trust you must be very quiet and very calm, never move quickly or suddenly.

Perhaps this is the most important rule that we can learn in our dealings with horses and ponies. If only people can remember this, then they will be able to have lots of fun and happiness and success with all sorts of different ponies and horses – for the whole of a lifetime.

ALL SORTS OF BREEDS

The original horse was probably only about 24 inches high; that is to say, about the size of a foxhound. He was very strong and fast, and as we have said he lived in a herd. Often he was chased and hunted by bigger animals. So, like most animals that are hunted, he still has eyes at the side of his head: whereas the animals that hunt, the predatory animals as they are called, such as the fox, the hawk, and man, have eyes placed at the front of the head.

It is because the original horse was so often pursued that he is by nature nervous and high-strung. It is always interesting how the qualities of an animal survive through thousands of years and generations.

The original horse was very tough and so it is the smaller breeds that are tough today, rather than the very beautiful but less natural and much bigger thoroughbreds. Not surprisingly the horses and ponies that live in the more severe climates of the north are the toughest of all. One can imagine the sturdy little Przewalski (page 12, top), the animal most like the original horse, in the Gobi desert or the icy steppes of Russia. In thousands of years he seems hardly to have changed at all. He could survive the hard conditions of the frozen north, apparently existing on very little.

Almost equally hardy is the famous Shetland (shown below left) who comes from the far north of the British Isles. He is extremely strong too, and though he is very friendly he can sometimes have a mind of his own. He is the smallest of all the well-known British breeds of ponies, but is not in fact the smallest pony in the world.

In South America there is a breed of small horse, sometimes only 9 hands high (there are 4 inches in a hand), called Falabella. They are very attractive little animals and lovely for very young children to ride – except that you feel you might want to take one to bed, like a toy!

There are nine British breeds of ponies. They are: Connemara, Dartmoor, Dale, Exmoor, Fell, Highland, New Forest, Shetland, and the Welsh, (like the one opposite).

It is because the British Isles is lucky enough to have all these different types of ponies that there are more suitable ponies for children here to ride than in any other country. In some countries on the Continent there are no ponies at all, so their children cannot begin to ride until they are big enough to ride horses. The result of this is that many ponies bred in Britain are exported to other countries, and so British ponies became famous all over the world. But other countries do have their own ponies, such as the Norwegian pony with her foal, below.

One usually thinks of ponies as animals to ride, but in many countries they are more often driven, either pulling a cart or a sleigh. This is because in such countries the terrain is not suitable for riding, the ground may be uneven and is often dangerous. This means that horses and ponies must keep to the roads and tracks, which for riding is rather uninteresting: but as they are often steep, walking is hard work. Then it is much nicer to be pulled along in a cart or on a sledge.

Obviously a pony that is used between shafts must have a perfect temperament. If a pony shies it is possible to control him fairly easily if you are riding him; but if he shies when he is being driven, it is much harder to control him. Then if he really got out of control he might turn the cart or sledge over, which could be very dangerous.

The Haflinger, like the one shown opposite, comes from Austria. It is not only a lovely pony to look at with its long mane and tail and bright chestnut colour, but it also has an ideal temperament and is very strong, as is the sturdy Icelander we show below.

The beautiful ponies in the New Forest are very different from the sturdy ponies in Northern Europe. See how attractive the little foal opposite is. They are so friendly people want to talk to them and feed them at the side of the road. This is not a good thing, as they get into the habit of wandering on to the road and on a dark night they can easily be hit by a car. A large number of New Forest ponies are killed or injured by cars every year.

Sometimes, too, a pony that has learned to expect titbits from visitors gets annoyed if someone comes along who does not feed him. Then he can turn quite nasty: so this is another reason why it is not kind to feed them.

Each year the agisters – the pony keepers in the New Forest – round the ponies up and count them, then a certain number of them are sold. The New Forest is still one of the most attractive of all British ponies: also the most popular. Many people think he is the ideal child's pony, because he has a very good temperament – though goodness knows what he would say if he had a koala bear on his back, like the Australian pony below!

As well as the different breeds there are distinctive types such as the lovely Palomino and her foal, below. Sometimes it is known as the Golden Horse, or in Spain as Ysabella. As well as the magnificent gold of its chestnut coat it has a white mane and tail, but no white anywhere else, except on the face. It is descended from the Arab and always looks very smart, under saddle, between shafts or in a parade.

Another type is the 'coloured' horse or pony, a piebald or a skewbald. A piebald is black and white: a skewbald is brown and white. Many breeds can be piebalds or skewbalds as well as plain colours, like the Dartmoor mare, opposite, with her foal.

The Dartmoor may look a little more elegant than the Fell above her, but the Fells are very popular in the north. They are wonderfully comfortable to ride, and are very surefooted. The Fell is probably the easiest of all the breeds to recognise, usually jet black with a long, flowing mane and tail of fine and silky hair. They stand about 13 h.h. which means they are ideal for children of about eleven or twelve: they are also very suitable for elderly people as they are so safe.

It is not only in parts of Britain that there are herds of ponies. You see below a herd of wild ponies in Virginia, in the United States of America. Once a year they are rounded up and sold at an average price of 75 dollars: that is about £30. After their wild life in the herd they tame very quickly, and are good, cheap children's ponies.

It must seem strange at first coming out of the herd and being all on their own, but this wise old lady opposite seems quite content, untroubled by the fly on her nose.

I would be happier if she did not have barbed wire round her field. It is so dangerous.

WORK
AND PLAY

Riding for most people is either work or play. However much fun it is for a jockey, every ride is work. For the mounted sentry on guard in Whitehall, riding is work. For the mounted police officer, riding is work. But when a child takes part in a gymkhana it is play: to go pony trekking is play: hunting is play. But the Pony Club is both work and play, for in addition to all the fun, the mounted games, the mock hunt, there is the work, the learning to ride, the learning to look after a pony, the learning how to instruct.

The Pony Club was founded in 1929. At first there were only three branches. Now in Britain there are well over 300 and in other countries nearly 800. Altogether there are over 100,000 members: and since 1929 there have been more than a million members.

The objects of the Pony Club are:
* to encourage young people to learn to ride and to learn to enjoy all kinds of sport connected with horses and riding;
* to provide instruction and to instil in members knowledge of the proper care of their animals;
* to promote the highest ideals of sportsmanship, citizenship and loyalty, thereby cultivating strength of character and self-discipline.

One of the most popular times of the Pony Club year is when the Pony Club Camp is held in the summer holidays. It is equally successful and popular in Britain and overseas: indeed with the more reliable weather, as in Australia for instance, a Pony Club Camp like the one in the top picture opposite, is more likely to be run successfully than in the uncertain weather in Britain.

A good Pony Club always insists on both pony and rider being well turned-out. Some children even like their pony to be extra smart with a coloured brow band.

A hard hat should always be worn, especially when jumping, because it is a protection for the head, not only if you should fall but also if, having fallen, your pony should by mistake kick you.

25

One expects a pony to look well and happy if it belongs to a member of a Pony Club, as, indeed, do the ponies at this Pony Club rally in Australia opposite (top); and even more the beautiful ponies below them, shown at the famous Royal International Horse Show in London; but a pony can also look well if it is living a far more humble life like this coster's pony below. There is a special charm about the companionship of man and animal working together, and the costers are perhaps the only traders still to be seen touring the city streets with horse-drawn carts.

You will seldom see a coster's pony looking anything but well and happy. After all, the coster depends on his pony for his living. If he is going to do as much as twenty or even thirty miles a day, all on hard roads, then obviously it is essential that the pony is fit and sound. His legs especially must be really hard, otherwise the roads will jar them to pieces and the coster will be left with a lame pony: but a pony that is lame still has to be fed, although it cannot work.

It is not only costers who drive ponies, and what is more you are never too young to start. So popular is driving now, even with children, that many of the big shows have driving classes and often quite small children can be seen taking part in them.

One does not very often nowadays see girls riding side-saddle. But how elegant and dignified they can look. Nor is it as difficult as it looks. Often ladies who ride side-saddle will tell you that it is much more difficult to fall off than if you are riding astride, because there is a pommel to hold the lower leg in place, and a second pommel which is gripped by the upper leg.

Today riding is one of the most popular forms of recreation. About half a million people ride in Britain today, and in one state alone in the United States – California – riding is almost equally popular, so you can imagine how many people ride in the whole of America, let alone in all the other countries in the world. I doubt if anyone thought that riding would remain so popular when cars and aeroplanes were invented. But in fact it is more popular than ever before, just because it is such a wonderful pastime, whether it is pony trekking or taking part in a gymkhana or just hacking.

Mind you, as the mare and foal opposite prove, it can be great fun just being a horse or pony enjoying a good gallop. These two are at the Greater London Council establishment at Hainault where ponies are trained to provide children's rides in London parks. Foals in particular are so full of the joy of living that they love to gallop just for the sake of galloping. Perhaps they know that before long they will have a bit in the mouth and a saddle on the back. Then they will only gallop when they're told to.

In some countries trotting races are more popular than ordinary races. It may be hard to believe, but in fact a trotter going flat out can go just about as fast as a horse going full speed at the gallop.

One rather strange thing when driving a trotter is that the harder the driver pulls, the faster the trotter will go. When you want him to stop you ease on the reins.

Not surprisingly, in countries where trotting is popular children take it up at an early age, like these two in the United States. Children also have the advantage of being lightweight.

The little cart in which they drive is called a sulky. It is a funny little skeleton of a cart with two wheels and long shafts. The driver generally sits on a padded bar, not a seat at all, and he has his legs sticking almost straight out in front of him, pushing against steel rings. It never looks very comfortable, but those who trot, say that jockeys riding short do not look very comfortable and maybe they are right!

Although trotting has never become very popular in Britain, there are sometimes demonstrations like the one below in the beautiful show ground at Balmoral, in Ulster.

In trotting races two kinds of horses are used: those which trot, that is, their legs move diagonally, the off-fore with the near-hind and the near-fore with the off-hind; and those which pace, that is, those which move the off-fore and off-hind together and then the near-fore and the near-hind together, like a camel.

It is said that over long distances the latter is a very comfortable gait. This may be true, because hundreds of years ago the pilgrims riding to Canterbury made their horses use this gait. It was then called ambling.

Trotting racing is one thing, but the ordinary rider should always remember that a horse should never be made to trot fast. The trot should always be at a collected pace and only occasionally, as in dressage, extended.

There could hardly be a greater contrast between the pits down a coal mine and the bright lights of a circus.

At the end of the last world war in 1945, there were more than 20,000 ponies like this one in our picture used in the pits. Now there are less than a quarter of that number.

A hundred years ago the work done by ponies in the pits used to be done by women and children. Only when an Act of Parliament stopped this were ponies employed.

The story that pit ponies go blind is untrue. On the contrary, they are very well cared for; each keeper treats his pony as though it were his own pet. They often live a long life and at the end when they are retired they go out to good farms. This is arranged by the National Coal Board or by the R.S.P.C.A.

Circus ponies, too, are very well looked after. They do so much travelling they probably have a more exhausting life than a pit pony. The funny spotted pony in the picture is a Danish breed: he is jumping a skewbald Shetland.

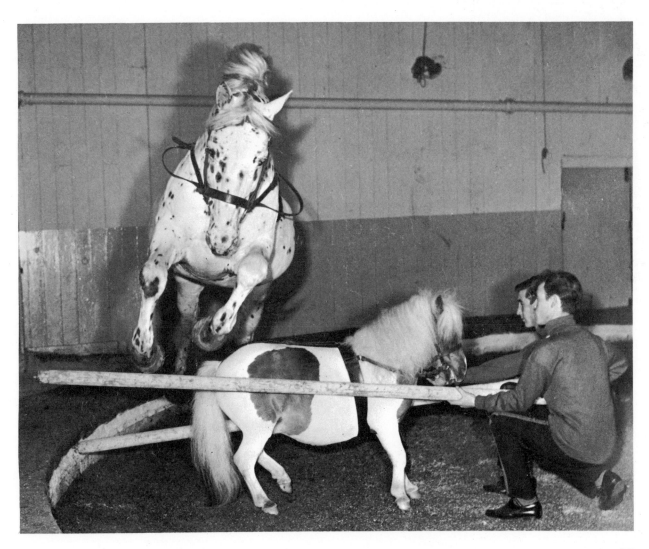

Some people will suggest that a pony can only be taught to perform in a circus by cruel training. This is not true. If there were any cruelty in the training, a pony would become frightened and never have the confidence vital for him to be able to perform correctly.

Confidence is so very important in a performing pony, whether it is in a circus or over jumps. It is when a pony is frightened that he does silly things. Often people complain that they cannot catch a pony or cannot make him go into his box or trailer. The reason is really quite simple. At some time or another the pony has been frightened, and instinctively he will try to avoid anything that he associates with something unpleasant.

Incidentally, it is very important that a horse or pony should never be driven fast in a trailer. Sometimes one has seen a trailer swaying all over the road because of the rate it is being driven. Just imagine what it must be like for the poor pony inside. No wonder he is sometimes frightened.

It does not matter where they are, a pony and its rider can be as one. Not a care in the world, placid, happy, content like the Iranian boy and the American girl in our pictures. If, of course, a rosette has been won then it is more exciting; but even the peace of the wide open spaces can have its own excitement.

Not every pony is beautiful, but that does not matter very much as long as it is well cared for. If a pony has a nice paddock of at least two acres, it will not need much feeding as the grass will be sufficient for it all through the summer months. In the winter it will need hay. But if it is kept inside, the pony wants hard food as well, such as oats.

There is always something very romantic about Romanies, the correct name for gipsies. Often they are associated with the more old-fashioned circuses; but now even those seem to have motor-drawn caravans – very different from the real old covered wagons.

If you are lucky enough to be able to see inside a Romany caravan you will see how well-equipped and comfortable it is. It is amazing how much can be put into such a small space.

Most Romanies take great pride in their caravans and keep them gay and shining. They are also natural and very good horse-masters. You will never see a Romany pony that is not well cared for and in good condition.

Even if you are rather small it is nice to feel that you can give your pony a titbit quite confidently, knowing that it will not think of biting you. Perhaps it makes you feel a little grand and possessive; but what is really wrong with that?

Anyway, if a pony is going for a long ride it needs plenty to eat. Trekkers do up to twenty miles a day, and more. Most of it, of course, is not very fast: but then who would want to hurry in such beautiful scenery as this round Llanrhaidr in North Wales? More and more people are taking to pony trekking as the ideal way to spend a summer holiday: always hoping that the weather will be kind and the saddle not too hard!

One has heard of seahorses, but one does not usually associate horses with bathing! In fact not only does it do horses good to have a splash, but they enjoy it. Although the sea itself is very good for horses' legs, more likely it is the firm sand and the hard work of pushing through the water that is really likely to do the horses good.

Very few horses dislike water. It is just a question of introducing them to it in a sensible way. Certainly it must be very refreshing for them. Just think how the horses opposite would love a splash after twenty miles or so under the relentless sunshine of Arizona. All the same, that lovely blue sky must be some compensation for the heat there.

Trekking can be really rewarding wherever you ride – in Scotland or in Wales, or in English Yorkshire, but it must be a particularly wonderful experience to trek in the great wide open spaces of the middle West. No wonder it is such a popular sport. Fortunately there are plenty of horses and ponies that are ideal for the job. And there is certainly no doubt that they are in great demand.

Stand at ease! It does not matter what a pony is doing, it is always pleasant to have a rest. Incidentally there is always a danger of children working their ponies too hard, especially at gymkhanas. Not only do they never get off their backs, but while they are uninvolved they use their ponies as a grandstand, sitting on their backs all the time, instead of getting off and giving their ponies a rest – not forgetting to loosen their ponies' girths. This thoughtlessness can cause the ponies undue strain. After all, for a human being it is as easy to stand as to sit, and really not very much more tiring: but it is much more of a relief for a pony to lose a weight of eight or nine stone from its back.

Mind you, to ride through such lovely scenery as on the right, in sunny Australia, at a lazy pace in the sunshine must be restful in itself.

And though it must be something of an ordeal for the little Icelandic pony, a mascot of the Royal Guards Regiment in Copenhagen, he too has his off-duty moments.

To think that some people can dress up and ride horseback in this wonderful regalia and it is not considered a fancy dress. Isn't this Indian Chief magnificent?

Very different are the Scottish gipsy women below. This picture was taken some years ago, but the essentials of gipsy life are the same today. Their life is certainly simple enough, but it is good and satisfying. Their ponies are hardy and well cared for: moreover they are trusty and reliable. On either side they carry paniers – so called from the French word meaning basket.

The gipsies walk as far as the ponies do themselves. That is why they, too, always look fit and hardy – and content. Scotland is so beautiful a country that there must be many town dwellers who would be more than satisfied to wander round the beautiful lochs, making their way from village to village selling their wares, as the gipsies have done for hundreds of years.

That really is the point. Man can now fly to the moon; you and I can travel from one end of the world to the other at just about the speed of sound, and yet the horse still has his function and his uses: and he goes at exactly the same speed as he did two, three, ten thousand years ago.

CARE OF YOUR PONY

Nobody who rides must ever forget that it is privilege to ride. A pony or a horse is not just a machine, like a motorbicycle: it is flesh and blood like you and me. It has to be properly and carefully looked after. It has to be regularly fed and, equally important, it must always have water. It must never be allowed to get too cold. But when it is very hot the pony must have enough shade, and be protected from the flies.

It has teeth which grow and which from time to time must be tended. In fact the animal's teeth can tell a lot about its age and health. It is most important to check this when buying a new pony. Always call in a veterinary man or horse expert to undertake this for you. Never rely on your own judgement or that of an enthusiastic amateur, or you could find yourself with a sick animal or one that is older than you thought. It has hooves which grow as do human being's finger or toe nails, and these also must constantly be attended to. A horse or a pony must never be taken for granted, because it cannot speak. It cannot tell you when it is feeling unwell: but like human beings it can just as easily have its off days. A lack-lustre eye, a sluggish outlook, will tell you all is not well. The good horsemaster learns to recognise these things, and will be on the look out for them.

The worst enemy is ignorance. There is always so much to learn about horses and ponies. Indeed one can never get to the end of learning. The person who begins by thinking he knows it all, is soon going to find how little he really knows.

Every horse and every pony is different. Not only are they different in their size and ability, but they are different in their temperament and their requirements. It is up to the owner to know just what the needs of his or her particular animal are.

In fact there are few things more rewarding than getting to know your pony thoroughly. It is even more rewarding when you establish a complete understanding with your pony. This should be every rider's goal.

It is rather annoying when, just as you think you are managing perfectly, an older sister or somebody else who thinks she knows everything comes along and decides that you must be led. As if one were not perfectly capable of managing by oneself! They always want to show off and be bossy!

It is, of course almost equally annoying when you are left by yourself and, without your wanting it to, your pony decides to help itself to a mouthful of grass, or even bush or shrubbery. Why do ponies have to be so obstinate?

Ponies can be a little obstinate and a little headstrong. This is because, being small, they are usually broken-in without being properly ridden. On the other hand, they are easy by nature, and a child, if he or she is firm, should be able to teach a pony discipline without very much difficulty.

The important thing is to establish very definitely who is boss. If the rider is boss the pony soon accepts it: but he is quite ready to be boss himself if he is given the chance.

Most people feel that a pony sale is a bit of a shambles. Sometimes one worries lest the ponies are being ill-treated. There is no real cause for alarm. They are not at the sale for long and then the majority of the ponies go to good homes.

What do we mean by a good home? There can be no doubt that a good home is where it is realised that nothing is more important than proper stable-management. This not only means proper care and treatment of the tack in the saddle-room: tack which is well looked after is less likely to be uncomfortable for a pony. It also means knowing how to fit it correctly.

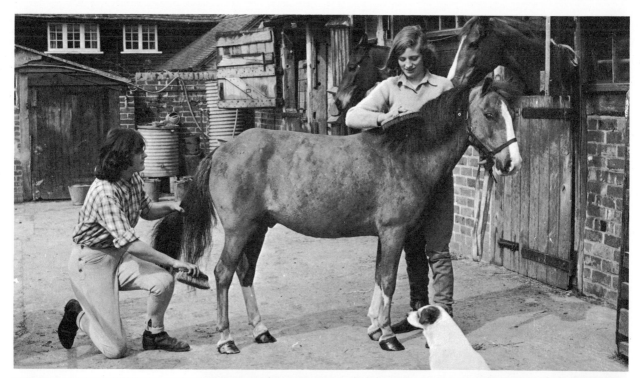

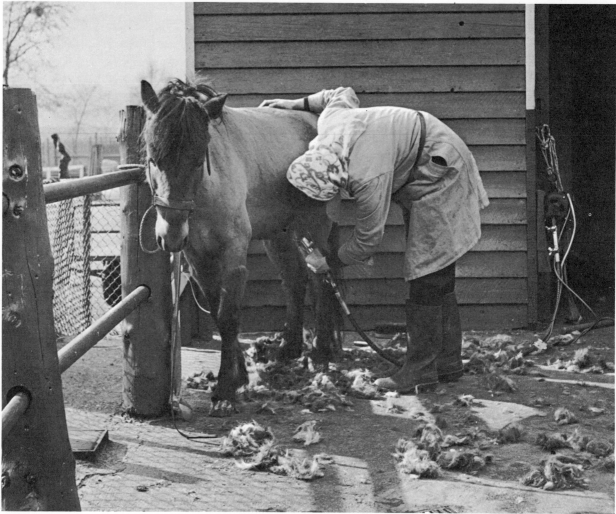

Proper care of a horse or pony also means the grooming of it. Grooming does not just mean running over the pony with a body-brush. There is much more to it than that. It means properly cleaning the pony. One of the less easy things is the pulling of the mane and tail, but it is worth doing this well because it can make a pony look very smart. In the show ring it can make all the difference.

If a pony is kept in in the winter and is being worked, then it will have to be clipped. The winter coat is so thick that it would be most uncomfortable for a pony to work in it – like playing tennis in a fur coat!

Most ponies do not mind the clipping machine. They rather like the whirr of the blades. But occasionally if a pony has been frightened by having its hair pulled or, worse, received a shock from the clippers, then it may be difficult and you will have to be very careful, especially round the head.

'Yes, I *have* cleaned my teeth!'

58

As with most things there are both the skilled and the ordinary, everyday jobs to be done with horses.

To get a horse fit and well-balanced he can be 'lunged', as shown in our picture. But this is a skilled exercise and should not be practised by those who do not know how to do it correctly.

Mucking-out, on the other hand, requires no great skill, but is hard work. Probably, however, it is the most basic essential connected with care of horses. A stable that is not clean is a bad stable. A horse or pony that is dirty is a joy neither to its rider nor itself.

If a pony is kept in a stable then the day must always start with the mucking-out. There is one thing that should be considered more important and that is to see that the pony has water. Then of course, it has to be fed. But that mucking-out just cannot be avoided – so that you had better get down to it!

And if all these things are remembered, well, you may be as successful a horseman as this little chap. And as confident as the one over the page!

ACKNOWLEDGEMENTS

Colour
Camera Press, 36 bottom, 37, 44; Canadian Government Travel Bureau 48; Tom Parker 41; Photo Researchers 8, 9; Picturepoint 45; Peter Roberts 36 top; Syndication International 33, 40; Z.F.A. 12 top, 12 bottom, 16.

Black and White
Animal Photography 15, 50; Godfrey Argent 38; Australian News and Information Bureau 24 top, 27 top, 47 top; Peter Baker 43; Thorbjorn Bakken 14; Barnaby's Picture Library 18, 21 bottom, 24 bottom, 39; Camera Press 22, 58 bottom; Camera Talks 54 bottom; Fox Photos 29, 31 top, 60; E. O. Hoppe 17; Keystone Press Agency 47 bottom, 54 top; Miles Brothers 21 top; Monty 27 bottom; Tierbilder Okapia 57; Press Association 56 top, 59; Tom Parker 20, 23; Roger Perry 28; Pictorial Press 10, 11, 19, 31 bottom, 32; Popperfoto 34, 49; Peter Roberts 58 top; The Scottish Tourist Board 30, 42, 46; Sport and General Press Agency 35; Nicholas Toyne 52, 53; Thomas A. Wilkie 26, 55.